# DESTINATION DESSERTS

*Treats That Travel To the Ones You Love*

## Kathleen Edmunds, MD

WestBow Press books may be ordered through booksellers or by contacting:

WestBow Press
A Division of Thomas Nelson & Zondervan
1663 Liberty Drive
Bloomington, IN 47403
www.westbowpress.com
1 (866) 928-1240

ISBN: 978-1-4908-8253-6 (sc)
ISBN: 978-1-4908-8254-3 (e)

Library of Congress Control Number: 2015909164

Print information available on the last page.

WestBow Press rev. date: 6/17/2015

WESTBOW
PRESS
A DIVISION OF THOMAS NELSON
& ZONDERVAN

# CONTENTS

# INTRODUCTION

One of the hardest times a mother can experience emotionally is having her children leave for college. When my first son, Meade, left home for college in another state it was hard coming downstairs every morning and not seeing his smiling face. Even worse was pulling in or out of the driveway and not seeing his car, a second reminder jolt! When his birthday came around I wanted to send him a Birthday Cake. After searching on-line I finally settled on a Shipped Carrot Cake that cost me over $90.00! When he received it he simply said it was "ok, but not as good as yours." Another jolt to my heart. I have always made a huge deal out of my kid's birthdays, usually spanning a Birthday Week, so this was a total let down. I wanted to send him something that was delicious, pleasurable, and memorable of home and didn't cost almost $100.00!

I started thinking about my most popular desserts, ones that my kids and all their friends love. These recipes come from a few places. Some come from my Mom and Grandmothers, who started me baking at a very young age. Most of these are recipes I have received from friends, where I've tried something they brought to a potluck and said "that's great! Can I have the recipe?" Or by modifying one of the hundreds of recipes from School Cookbooks that I have been coerced into buying (either by the schools my kids were attending at the time or a child or mother hawking them at my door as a fundraiser for their school.) In Tennessee, I also get plenty of exposure to church, neighborhood or company cookbooks, which usually my patients give to me or want me to buy from them. Also, I read the local newspaper where our very own Mary Constatine is always putting in a new delectable recipe she has found. Last but not least, I'm always in a bookstore to peruse the latest cookbook. Then I started thinking of how to ship it. As a practicing OB/GYN, pharmaceutical companies are always bringing "drug lunches" to my office in Steamer Pans, so I will prescribe their drugs to my patients. But these Steamer Pans got me thinking and I found them with Metal Lids that you buy in large quantities at Sam's for cheap. So I started making cakes in Steamer Pans, but they were so heavy that shipping them by FED EX or UPS was expensive. Then I found the US Postal Service Medium Priority Shipping Box that " if it Fits it Ships anywhere in the U.S." for $12.65, usually in 2 days. You can also always mail these any day of the week because the boxes and shipping are available at most U.S. Post Offices 24 hours a day! I was on my way! When you go to the post office to ship these, they always ask if it is perishable. Just answer no. This is so they can put a sticker on the box that says perishable. If you answer yes it is perishable at the 24 hour automated center, it will not let you mail it. I have asked and been reassured by several postal agents that you can ship baked goods in these boxes.

I am a practicing OB/GYN, married to a Gastroenterologist, with 3 kids ages 23, 21 and 17. Because of this I have an endless supply of guinea pigs for my recipes. I bring desserts several times a week to my office where my nurses are always on some form of diet, but they will always try at least a taste (and usually more) of what I bring in. One of my patients recently told me that if she was going to jump off the Weight Watchers wagon then she wanted to use her points on something that was "incredible"! Those are the words she used to describe the Blueberry, Cream Cheese Ouie Gooie Cake. My Ultrasonographer, as an Advocare rep., is the hardest to crack. Every day I bring in a dessert, she takes a picture and puts it on Facebook with a notation saying, "This is today's temptation." I take desserts several times a month into Labor and Delivery at St. Mary's, where I have practiced for 19 years. I also send them to one of my husband's three offices for holidays or special occasions. My oldest son, Meade, graduated last year from Hampden-Sydney College in Virginia majoring in Chemistry. So shipping cakes to him were always a hit on the Chemistry floor or in the dorm. When Meade came from the Post Office with a Shipping Box everyone came out to see what I had sent and get a bite! My daughter, Shannon, is a senior at the University of Georgia majoring in Finance. She lives in a house with two other girls and they discourage me from sending "fattening" desserts, but they can always take a bite and send it over to her sorority house, Kappa Kappa Gamma. My youngest son, Carter, is a senior in high school. (I know, I'm almost an empty nester!) I don't know a high school teacher or student who doesn't appreciate a yummy dessert. Last but not least, my father lives in Williamsburg, VA and entertains almost every evening. He built a 12 chair, multi-level theater in his attic and streams in the Metropolitan Opera! I ship him mostly Carrot Cakes and Whiskey Cakes. When I first started sending my dad cakes, I told him it was my way of coping with my children leaving. I could not believe their childhoods had passed so quickly. He reminded me that I had only lived with him 18 years of his Life!

I have 50 Cookbooks in my house, but each one only has a few recipes that are **awesome and shippable**. The rest of the recipes are ok or even downright awful. A pet peeve of mine is that most of these cookbooks lack pictures of their recipes. They contain pages and pages of print, but I want to see what they look like! You would have to make everything in the book to find the one or two **great** items. I think the best way to make a dessert is to first gather up all the ingredients before you start. I don't know how many times I have started to make something, and half way through I realize I have no eggs or my milk is spoiled. This way, you know you have everything before you start. I also don't know how many cookbooks I have destroyed the pages with batter, so wipeable pages are a must! Putting them on your electronic device is fine, but I'm tired of getting flour and sugar in the crevices. I wanted to make a cookbook that any Baker could make yummy desserts and ship them to their kids in college or whoever might love a treat. I do not make any promises that any of these desserts are healthy or beautiful to look at (there is nothing worse than a BEAUTIFUL cake that tastes HORRIBLE!), but most are easy to make, portable, shippable and make it hard to take just one bite. Your child will be a hit in the Dorm and they will continuously experience a little bit of home!

# WINTER SHIPPERS

The first recipe I want to start with is the Strawberry Cake. This recipe was given to me by one of my employees many years ago. She brought it to the office. I took one bite and said "I have to have that recipe!" It is very sweet, very strawberry and very, very moist. It's hard to cut a piece; you almost have to scoop it out with a spoon.(Strawberry Cake is a dessert that when you order it at a restaurant you are hoping for this cake but invariably get a dry, slightly strawberry tasting layer cake.) I was recently at the Post Office shipping a Strawberry Cake to my oldest son the week before he graduated from Hampden-Sydney College when another mother approached me and asked me what I was shipping. When I told her she said "I should have thought of that when my kids were in college!" Many of my kids friends count this Strawberry Cake as their favorite and have their moms make it for their birthdays. At my younger son's Confirmation, a woman behind me asked me for the recipe, before the service even started. Her daughter was in my son's class the day before when he brought this Strawberry Cake in and she told her mom it was the best cake she had ever eaten! You may be asking how this recipe is different than the Cake Doctor version. They are similar in two respects- a white cake mix and strawberry gelatin. The Cake Doctor is a much drier version and using fresh strawberries (unless maybe in peak season) gives less flavor to me. The ingredients for this cake can be kept readily available in the cupboard and freezer.

## STRAWBERRY CAKE

Gather Up: 1 Box of White Cake Mix, 1 Large Box of Strawberry Gelatin, water, Vegetable Oil, 2 Eggs, Vanilla, 1 Stick of soft Butter, Confectioner's Sugar, frozen Strawberries

Mix in a large bowl:

    1 box of White Cake Mix

    1 large box of Strawberry Gelatin

    ½ cup of Water

    ½ cup of Vegetable Oil

    2 Eggs

    1 ½ teaspoons of Vanilla

Add:

      ¾ Cup of thawed, and Chopped Frozen Strawberries as described

Microwave for 2 minutes an overfilled 1 cup measuring cup of Sliced or Whole Frozen Strawberries. Using scissors cut the Strawberries up in the cup into small ¼ inch pieces. They should then measure about ¾ of a cup. Add them, juice and all to the above mixture.

Spray Pam into Steamer Pan 8x12

Pour Strawberry Cake batter into Pan and bake at 350 degrees for 40 minutes.

When you take the cake out the top will look pink and brown.

Punch small holes in the cake all over the top with a wooden toothpick or shish kabob skewer.

Cool cake completely.

Then Frost with Strawberry Frosting.

STRAWBERRY FROSTING

Mix in a medium bowl:

      1 stick (1/2 cup) of softened butter

      1 teaspoon of Vanilla

      4 Cups of Powdered Sugar (1 Box)

      ½ Cup of thawed and chopped frozen Strawberries (as described above)

# HUMMINGBIRD CAKE

Gather Up: 3 Ripe Bananas, Vegetable Oil, Vanilla, 3 Eggs, Bisquick, Sugar, 1 Can of Crushed Pineapple in its own juice, Chopped Pecans, Flaked Coconut

Mix in a Large Bowl:

   3 Ripe (black) Bananas cream with a fork

   1/3 Cup of Vegetable Oil

   1 teaspoon of Vanilla

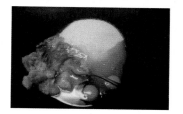

   3 Eggs

   2 ½ Cups of Bisquick

   1 Cup of Sugar

   1 large can (16 oz) Crushed Pineapple in its own Juice. Do Not Drain.

   ½ Cup Chopped Pecans

   1 Cup of Flaked Coconut

Spray Pam into a Steamer Pan.

Pour Hummingbird Cake Batter into Pan and bake at 350 degrees for 45 minutes.

Cool Cake Completely.

Frost with Cream Cheese Frosting.

CREAM CHEESE FROSTING:

Gather Up: 8 oz of softened Cream Cheese, softened Butter, Powdered Sugar and Vanilla

In a medium size bowl mix:

   1 (8oz) packages of softened Cream Cheese

   1 Stick of Butter softened (1/2 Cup)

Add:

   4 Cups of Sifted Powdered Sugar, 1 teaspoon of Vanilla

Beat with spoon until smooth. You will think that it never will mix and become frosting, but keep mixing and it does! People love anything I put this Cream Cheese Frosting on!!!!

The Glazed Carrot Cake is a recipe from my good friend, Rhonda. Whenever I get a slice of carrot cake at a restaurant, it always turns out to be a slice of dry, spice cake. This includes The Cheesecake Factory. They really know how to make Cheesecake but their expensive version of Carrot Cake is dry and tasteless. This recipe is a wonderful, flavorful Carrot Cake! The buttermilk glaze is so good you want to eat it with a spoon. The glaze adds to an already moist cake and the cream cheese frosting accentuates the glaze. This is the ultimate double frost cake! My husband likes this cake stacked but when I ship it, I put it in a steamer pan. In the steamer pan I only glaze the top. The first time I shipped it I was worried that is would get broken up in the shipping. Rhonda confided in me that one time, right before her guests were going to arrive for a garden club luncheon, she tripped and spilled a stacked carrot cake on her clean kitchen floor. Always industrious, she grabbed a big glass bowl, scooped the cake up and served it with a spoon. Her guests raved about how good it was never realizing it was, supposed to be a layer cake.

## GLAZED CARROT CAKE

Gather Up: 3 Eggs, Sugar, Vegetable Oil, Buttermilk, Vanilla, Flour, Baking Soda, Salt, Ground Cinnamon, 8 oz drained Crushed Pineapple, Chopped Pecans, Grated Carrots, Flaked Coconut, Butter, and Light Corn Syrup

Mix in a Large Bowl:

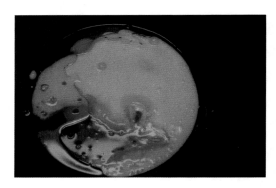

    3 large Eggs

    2 Cups of Sugar

    ¾ Cup of Vegetable Oil

    ¾ cup of Buttermilk

    2 teaspoons of Vanilla

Add:

    2 Cups of Flour (all-purpose or Ultragrain)

    2 teaspoons of Baking Soda

    ½ teaspoon of Salt

    2 teaspoons of Ground Cinnamon

Beat for 2 minutes with a hand mixer.

Add:

    1 (8 oz) can Crushed Pineapple (drained)

    2 Cups of Grated Carrots (fresh) I use Shredded Carrot Sticks you can buy at the store

    1 Cup of Flaked Coconut

    ½ Cup Chopped Pecans

Spray a Steamer Pan with Pam.

Pour Batter into Pan(s) making sure the carrots and coconut are evenly distributed.

Bake at 350 degrees. Steamer Pan for 50 minutes

These cakes will be very brown on top when done and a knife inserted in the center will come out clean.

Cool Cake(s) and then first frost with Buttermilk Glaze

BUTTERMILK GLAZE

Gather Up: Sugar, Buttermilk, Baking Soda, Butter, Light Corn Syrup and Vanilla

Mix in a small saucepan:

   3/4 cup Sugar

   1/3 Cup of Buttermilk

   1 teaspoon of Baking Soda

   1/3 Cup of Butter

   1 Tablespoon of Light Corn Syrup

Bring to a Boil over Medium heat. Boil for 4 minutes while stirring constantly until Glaze is Golden.

Remove from heat and stir in 1 teaspoon of Vanilla. Cool until the consistency of Syrup.

Pour Buttermilk Glaze evenly over cake. In a Steamer pan I only use Glaze on top or the Carrot Cake will be too moist. (YES that is possible! I made a HUGE Carrot Cake for my husband's large office once and poured 2 recipes of Buttermilk Glaze on it. It was swimming in Glaze!)

After the Glaze has cooled Frost with Cream Cheese Frosting.

I first had this Apple Cake when I was a first year medical student at the University of Virginia. The Dean of Students, Dr. Craig, made a point of having every first year medical student over to his house for dinner. He used to invite 10 students at a time on Friday night. Mrs. Craig always made the same dinner Chicken and Rice Casserole, Apple Cake and a Chocolate Cake. The Apple Cake was so good that the secretary for Dr. Craig had a stack of recipe cards on her desk for it. I liked it so much that I had a bakery in Charlottesville, Virginia make it for my wedding cake when my husband and I were married in UVA's Chapel in 1986! This cake is best if it's made with Granny Smith Apples. If you use the large apples then 5 will do. If you buy a bag of medium size apples then 6 are needed. Don't use a sweet apple like Red Delicious or Gala or your cake will be too sweet! When you are mixing the apple chunks into the batter, it is best to use your fingers like you would mix a meatloaf. This cake can be layered, Steamer Pan or cupcakes. If you layer it with Cream Cheese frosting then I recommend frosting only the middle and top. In the Steamer Pan version, you can frost with Cream Cheese and drizzle with Carmel Ice Cream Topping (One of my daughter's favorite cakes!). Also, you can top with the Brown Sugar Glaze I used on the Pineapple Right Side-Up Cake. Do not double frost this cake with the Brown Sugar Glaze and Cream Cheese Frosting: it is way too sweet and you can't even taste the glaze. You can also top this with the Butter Rum Sauce. It depends on what time of year you are shipping this as to the best topping to use.

## MRS. CRAIG'S APPLE CAKE

Gather Up: 2 Eggs, Vegetable Oil, Sugar, Flour, Ground Cinnamon, Vanilla, Baking Soda, Salt, Granny Smith Apples, Chopped Walnuts

In a Large Bowl Mix:

 2 Eggs

 ¾ Cup of Vegetable Oil

 2 cups of Sugar

 2 teaspoons of Vanilla

Add:

 2 cups of Flour (All Purpose or Ultragrain)

 2 teaspoons of Ground Cinnamon

 1 teaspoon of Baking Soda

 ¼ teaspoon of Salt

Add and Mix with Fingers:

 4 large or 5 Medium Granny Smith Apples Peeled, and chopped into 1 cm pieces

 ½ cup of Chopped Walnuts

Let Mixture Stand for a few minutes until the juice from the apples makes it easier to blend. Then mix one more time.

Spray a Steamer Pan

Pour batter into pan(s) and bake at 350 degrees. Steamer Pan for 45 minutes

Cool Completely.

Frosting Options:

1. Dust with Powdered Sugar (year round shipper)

2. Frost with Cream Cheese Frosting and drizzle with Caramel Apple Dip or Ice cream Topping (Winter Shipper)

3. Brown Sugar Glaze (year round shipper)

I'm not sure which I like better the Cream Cheese Frosting with Caramel Drizzle or Brown Sugar Glaze. All options are Absolutely Delicious!

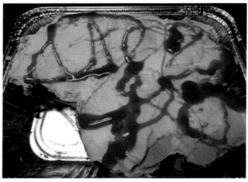

My husband and I spent our Internships and Residency in Rochester, New York at the University of Rochester, Strong Memorial Hospital. There we spent 4 years tasting some of the best Italian Cooking in the country! Although I am not a big fan of Cannoli's I really love a good moist Italian Cream Cake. This one is a family recipe of one of the Labor and Delivery Nurses that I have slightly doctored! The Amaretto gives it the perfect taste twang. Upstate New York is great wine country but I spent 1 ½ years of my 4 years there pregnant or nursing, so I was always the designated driver!

# AMARETTO ITALIAN CREAM CAKE

Gather Up: Butter, Flour, Coconut, Baking Soda, Vegetable Shortening, Sugar, 5 Eggs, Buttermilk, Amaretto Liquor and Chopped Walnuts

In a Large Mixing Bowl Cream:

> ½ Cup of Softened Butter (1 Stick)

> ½ Cup of Vegetable Shortening

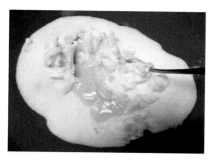

Add and Mix:

> 2 Cups of Sugar

> 5 Egg Yolks (Set Egg Whites aside)

Add:

> 1 Cup of Buttermilk

> 2 Cups of All Purpose Flour

> 1 teaspoon of Baking Soda

Mix in:

> 1/3 Cup of Amaretto

Fold In:

> 1 Cup of Sweetened Flaked Coconut

> ¾ Cup of Chopped Walnuts


Stiffly Beat 5 Egg Whites and Fold In.

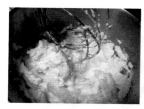 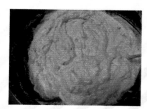

Pour Batter into (1) Steamer Pan sprayed with Pam.

Bake at 350 degrees for 40 minutes for a Steamer Pan

Cool

Frost with Cream Cheese Frosting

Frost Cooled Cake and Sprinkle top of cake with ½ Cup of Chopped Walnuts and ½ Cup of Sweetened Flaked Coconut

Blueberry, Cream Cheese Ouie Gooie Cake is not really a cake. You cannot cut it into slices and it can only be make in a Steamer Pan or 9x13. It is much better spooned out like a cobbler. You will see the basis of this cake in many cookbooks like the Cake Doctor's Gooey Butter Cake but this takes it one step further by adding fruit pie filling. The Blueberry cream cheese, Strawberry or Cherry cream cheese flavor combinations are incredible. Interestingly, Peach Pie filling makes it too sweet! If you just have to have Peaches, then I would cut up a fresh one and place on top. I suspect that canned peaches would also be too sweet. I found that decreasing the powdered sugar from 4 cups to 3 cups in the cream cheese layer makes it taste better when using fruit pie filling. Be sure not to over bake this one or the edge will get too hard. I saw this recipe melting the butter in the first step instead of using a pastry blender. I tried making it that way and it did not taste near as good as making it this way. It wasn't as Gooie!

## BLUEBERRY CREAM CHEESE OUIE GOOIE CAKE

Gather Up: Yellow Cake Mix, 3 Eggs, 1 Stick Butter, 8 oz Cream Cheese softened, Powdered Sugar and 1 Can of Berry Pie Filling(Blueberry, Cherry or Strawberry)

In a Medium Bowl Mix (A Pastry Blender or Fork works best. It will be lumpy like a bowl of peas.):

   1 Yellow Cake Mix

   1 Egg

   1 stick of Butter (leave hard Do Not Soften)

Pour this into a Steamer Pan sprayed with Pam.

In another Medium Bowl Mix:

   8 oz of soft Cream Cheese

   2 Eggs

   3 Cups of Powdered Sugar

Pour over Cake Mix

Then drop by large spoonfuls onto the Cream Cheese layer a Whole Can of Blueberry Pie Filling.

Bake at 350 degrees for 50 minutes. Don't Overbake! It Looks Gooie!!!!

This is the Cherry Pie Filling Version.

I like to make most cakes by scratch but sometimes you taste a doctored cake mix version that is hard to resist. I first tasted this at an end of season Football Banquet made with walnuts. I have had two sons play 8 years total of High School Football. I prefer to make it with Pecans and call it Chocolate Pecan Joy because it taste just like a pecan version of an Almond Joy Candy Bar! Every time I make this I am asked for the recipe after only one bite!

# CHOCOLATE PECAN JOY CAKE

Gather Up: One Chocolate Cake Mix, Vegetable Oil, Milk, Coarsely chopped Pecans, Coconut, Butter, 8 oz Cream Cheese, Powdered Sugar, and Semi- Sweet Chocolate Chips.

Mix:

Chocolate Cake Mix per the directions but use 1 cup of Milk instead of Water and set aside

(Most mixes are made with oil, eggs and water)

In a Medium bowl melt in the microwave on high for 2 minutes:

8 ounces of Cream Cheese and 1 stick (1/2 Cup) Butter

Add:

1 Box (4 Cups) of Confectioners' Sugar (it's a little hard to mix) set aside

  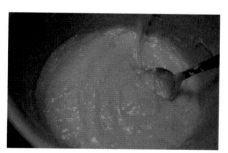

Spray a Shipper Pan with Pam.

Sprinkle 1 Cup of Coarsely Chopped Pecans on the bottom of the Pan.

Layer 1 ½ Cups of Shredded Sweetened Coconut on top of the nuts.

 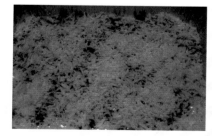

Spread HALF of the Chocolate Cake Mix Batter over Coconut Layer

Spread ALL of the Cream Cheese Mixture over the Cake Mix Batter

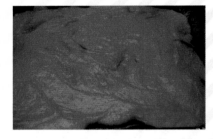

Top the Cream Cheese Layer with the other half of the Chocolate Cake Mix Batter

Top with 2 Cups of Semi-Sweet Chocolate Chips

Bake at 350 degrees for 45-50 minutes

Everyone in Tennessee seems to love Red Velvet Cake which is really a Chocolate Cake with Red Food Coloring. My youngest son Carter loves this Red Velvet Cake. This is one of the best Red Velvet Cake recipes I have tried. It is very moist. Of Course Frost it with my favorite Cream Cheese Frosting! It does not make good Cupcakes! Sorry!

# TENNESSEE RED VELVET CAKE

Gather Up: Sugar, Flour, Baking Soda, Cocoa, Buttermilk, Vegetable Oil, Eggs, White Vinegar, Vanilla and 1 oz. of Red Food Coloring

Put All the Ingredients In a Large Bowl in this Order and Mix:

    1 ½ Cups of Sugar

    2 ½ Cups of Flour (All Purpose)

    2 Teaspoon of Baking Soda

    1 ½ Tablespoons of Cocoa

    1 Cup of Buttermilk

    1 ½ Cup of Vegetable Oil

    2 Eggs

    1 Tablespoon of Vinegar

    1 Teaspoon of Vanilla

    1 oz. Red Food Coloring

Mix all together.

  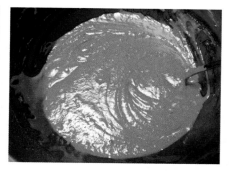

Pour into a Steamer Pan sprayed with Pam

Bake at 325 degrees for 45 minutes for a Steamer Pan.

Cool and Frost with Cream Cheese Frosting

The Pumpkin Brownies are the favorite of my sister- in -law, Anne who is an Operating Room nurse at Dartmouth College in New Hampshire. Yes, I ship them to her. Also, one of Meade's best friends in college, Damien counts these as his favorites. They both love these, and it's a good thing they are the ultimate shipper. They are very dense, moist and pumpkiny. If you dust with powdered sugar you can even ship these in the summer. I found this recipe in the school/church cookbook that has the Overnight Monkey Bread. See, every cookbook usually has 1 or 2 really Awesome recipes.

## PUMPKIN BROWNIES

Gather Up: Packed Pumpkin, Vegetable Oil, Sugar, Flour, 4 Eggs, Baking Powder, Ground Cinnamon and Salt

In a Large Bowl Mix:

    1 Can of Packed Pumpkin (15 oz)

    1 Cup of Vegetable Oil

    2 Cups of Sugar

    2 Cups of Flour (All Purpose or Ultragrain)

    4 Large Eggs

    1 teaspoon of Baking Powder

    1 teaspoon of Ground Cinnamon

    ½ teaspoon of Salt

Pour into a Steamer Pan sprayed with Pam. Bake at 350 degrees for 30 Minutes.

Cool.

Frost with Cream Cheese Frosting.

# EXTREME WINTER SHIPPERS

My son Meade's favorite cake is The Pumpkiny Cheese Cake. I have seen this recipe in several places including the Nestle cookbook, and different magazines. Originally, I saw this in a school cookbook. This tastes very similar to the Cheesecake Factory Pumpkin Cheesecake (I already said they make Great Cheesecake but really need to redo their Carrot Cake). It ships fine in a Steamer Pan, but only in the cold months with Ice Packs. Getting my Cheese Cake pan back has been difficult and it turns out perfect in a Steamer Pan! I would hate to smell the box if I shipped this cake over 2 days in 100 degree temperatures! Rotting Cream Cheese, UGH! By the way, the Nestle Cookbook breaks the rule of only 1-2 great recipes per cookbook. That cookbook is the Bomb! Almost every recipe in it is Awesome!

## PUMPKINY CHEESECAKE:

Gather Up: Butter, Graham Cracker Crumbs, Sugar, 24 oz of softened Cream Cheese, Light Brown Sugar, 2 Eggs, 1 can Pure Pumpkin, Evaporated Milk, cornstarch, Ground Cinnamon, Ground Nutmeg, 16 Oz Sour Cream and Vanilla

Crust:

In a small bowl mix:

½ Cup of Melted Butter

2 Cups of Graham Cracker Crumbs (If you only have whole crackers put 2 1/2 sleeves

In a Gallon size plastic bag and use a rolling pin to crush them into crumbs)

1/3 Cup of Sugar

Press onto bottom and 1 inch up the side of a Steamer Pan.

Bake at 350 degrees for 10 minutes.

Filling:

In a large bowl mix:

> 3 (8 oz) packages of softened Cream Cheese
>
> 1 cup of Sugar
>
> ¼ Cup of packed Light Brown Sugar
>
> 2 Large Eggs
>
> 1 (15 oz) can of Libby's 100% Pure Pumpkin
>
> 2/3 Cup of Evaporated Milk (5oz can)
>
> 2 Tablespoons of Cornstarch
>
> 1 teaspoon of Ground Cinnamon
>
> ½ teaspoon of Ground Nutmeg

Beat with a handheld electric mixer for 2 minutes.

Pour into Crust.

Bake at 350 degrees for 60 minutes.

Topping:

In a small bowl mix:

16 oz container of Sour Cream

1/3 Cup of Sugar

1 teaspoon of Vanilla

Pour on hot Cheesecake and put back in 350 degree oven for 10 more minutes.

Refrigerate for several hours. To ship I freeze it overnight and pack with two freezer packs on the bottom

The next 2 cakes I call Refrigerator Cakes. My Mom used to make something similar to these but I could never find her recipes. My husband brought the recipe for the Lemon version home one day from work. One of his nurses had brought it in and he told me it was the best cake he ever ate. Of course I had to make it! I must admit I am not a big fan of Lemon but I do like the Strawberry and Pina Colada versions. These taste best if left overnight in the refrigerator and are scooped out with a spoon. They can be layered in a Steamer Pan and Shipped in the Winter using two flat Icepacks one on top and one on the bottom. You can purchase Icepacks on Amazon for as little as fifty cents apiece depending on the quantity you buy. I also wrap these two cakes with plastic wrap and then put the metal lid on to prevent seepage while shipping

# PINA COLADA ICEBOX CAKE

Gather Up: 1 White Cake baked in a 9x13 pan, (1) 16 oz Cool Whip, 1 can of Bacardi's Frozen Pina Colada Mix, 1 Can of Sweetened Condensed Milk, a 20 ounce Can of Crushed Pineapple and Flaked Coconut

Mix and Bake a White Cake Mix in a 9x13 Pan according to the directions

Cool and Cut Into 2 inch Chunks

In a Large Bowl Mix:

    1 Large Cool Whip (16 0z)

    1 Can of Bacardis Frozen Pina Colada Mix (defrosted)

    1 Can of Sweetened Condensed Milk

Mix :

    1 ½ Cups of Sweetened Flaked Coconut

    20 ounce Can of Crushed Pineapple (Drained)

Layer in a Steamer Pan in the following order:

Filling, Coconut/pineapple, Cake, Filling, Coconut/pineapple, Cake, Filling, Coconut/pineapple

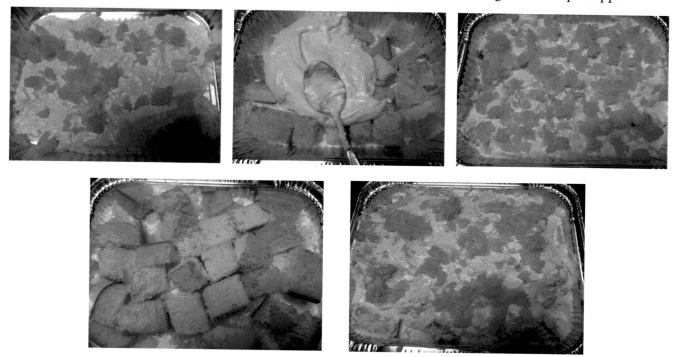

Refrigerate Overnight. Wrap with plastic wrap and then place metal lid on top.

Ship only in very cold weather with Ice packs on top and bottom.

# STRAWBERRY CREAM ICEBOX CAKE (This tastes just like Strawberry Shortcake!)

Gather Up: 1 White Cake baked in a 9X13 pan, (1) 16oz Cool Whip, 1 Jar of Strawberry Ice Cream Topping, 1 Can of Sweetened Condensed Milk, and Sliced Fresh Strawberries

Mix and Bake a White Cake Mix according to the directions

Cool and cut into 2 inch chunks

In a Large Bowl Mix:

>   1 Large Cool Whip (16 oz)

>   1 Jar of Strawberry Ice Cream Topping

>   1 Can of Sweetened Condensed Milk

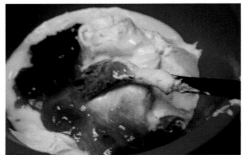

Set Aside:

>   2 Cups of Sliced Fresh Strawberries

Layer in a Steamer Pan in the following order:

>   Filling, Cake, Filling, strawberries, Cake, Filling and Top with strawberries

Refrigerate Overnight. Wrap with plastic wrap and then top with metal lid.

Ship only in very cold weather with Ice Packs on top and bottom of the shipping box.

The Following Bowl Cake is similar to the Icebox Cakes. The Dirt Cake is not even a cake but brownies. But, this is the "cake" my kids wanted brought to school for their birthday parties every year until almost 8th Grade! They are shippable in the winter using Ice Packs. I recently made this for the Senior Football Dinner and the boys basically licked the pan!

# DIRT CAKE

Gather Up: 1 pan of Brownies Baked, 1 Large Box of Instant Chocolate Pudding Mix, Milk, 16 oz Cool Whip, 1 Package of Double Stuff Oreo Cookies, Mini Chocolate Chips and Gummi Worms.

Bake 1 9x13 pan of Chocolate Brownies.

Cool and cut into 2 inch squares.

In a Medium Bowl Mix with Mixer until thick:

  1 Large package of Instant Chocolate Pudding Mix

  3 Cups of Milk

Place Whole Package of Double Stuff Oreo Cookies in a Gallon Size Plastic Bag.

Crush Cookies into crumbs with a Rolling Pin.

Layer in a Steamer Pan in the following order:

  Chocolate Pudding, ½ pan Brownies, Crushed Oreos, ¼ cup Mini Chocolate Chips, Cool Whip, ½ pan Brownies, Chocolate Pudding, Crushed Oreos, ¼ cup Mini Chocolate Chips, Cool Whip, Crushed Oreos and Gummi Worms

Refrigerate and Serve with a spoon. Wrap with plastic wrap and then top with metal lid when shipping.

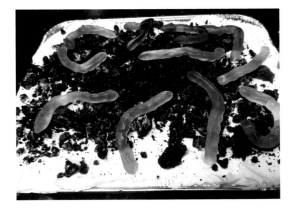

Ship only in very Cold weather using 2 ice packs in the shipping box.

# YEAR ROUND SHIPPERS

The Pineapple Right Side-Up Cake is my own creation. One of my good friends, Rhonda, is the mother of my oldest son's best friend, since age 4, Devon. She and I have toiled through many Halloween Carnivals, school holiday parties and birthday parties. When Meade was in high school he came home and told me Rhonda made the best Banana Bread in town! He could and did eat a whole loaf. Of course I had to call and get the recipe. It is a great, moist banana bread made with Bisquick and one recipe makes two loaf pans. This recipe became the backbone of 3 recipes in this book: Hummingbird Cake, Pineapple Right Side-Up Cake and Pineapple Cake. All 3 of these recipes are perfect in Steamer Pans. The Pineapple Right Side-Up Cake uses a whole can of crushed pineapple including the juice! There are several options to frost this cake, including a double-frost option. When you double frost a cake one frost is usually a glaze and the second a frosting. It is very important that either the glaze or the frosting is not very sweet. If both are sweet, then the cake is too sweet and you cannot discern between the two sweet tastes. In frosting the Pineapple Right Side-Up Cake, I prefer the brown sugar glaze alone. It tastes great but is not very pretty. Another option is just leaving it a Pineapple Cake and using Cream Cheese frosting. It tastes and looks great, but I'm a big fan of the pineapple-brown sugar combination. The Hummingbird variation of this cake involves mashing very ripe (black) bananas, a can of crushed pineapple in its own juice, coconut and chopped nuts. Cream cheese frosting is a must for a Hummingbird Cake! Remember to use very ripe bananas when baking bread, cakes or cupcakes. Yellow, normally ripe bananas are better in pies and banana pudding, but neither of these ship well.

## PINEAPPLE RIGHT SIDE UP CAKE

Gather Up: Vegetable Oil, Vanilla, 3 Eggs, Sugar, Bisquick, 1 Can of Crushed Pineapple in its own juice

Mix in a large bowl:

   1/3 Cup of Vegetable Oil

   1 teaspoon of Vanilla

   3 Eggs

   1 Cup of Sugar

   2 ½ Cups of Bisquick

   1 (16oz) can of Crushed Pineapple in its own juice. Do Not Drain.

Spray Pam into Steamer Pan.

Pour Pineapple Cake batter into Pan and bake at 350 degrees for 40 minutes

Punch small holes in the cake all over the top with a wooden toothpick or shish kabob skewer.

Cool the cake completely.

Frost with either Brown Sugar Glaze or Cream Cheese Frosting.

BROWN SUGAR GLAZE

Gather Up: Light Brown Sugar, Butter, Evaporated Milk and Vanilla

In a small saucepan mix:

    1 Cup of packed Light Brown Sugar

    4 Tablespoons of Butter (1/4 Cup)

    ¼ Cup of Evaporated Milk

Cook over medium-high heat. Boil and stir constantly for 2 minutes with a metal or wood spoon. Do Not Use a Whisk! Remove from heat and add 1 teaspoon of Vanilla. Pour over Cooled Cake.

My Daughter Shannon's second favorite cake is the Chocolate Cinnamon Cake. I have seen this in several school and church cookbooks. It is a moist chocolate cake with a touch of cinnamon and a to- die- for chocolate fudge frosting. You may have figured out by now that I am always modifying a recipe. Even if I love a recipe, I'll try to make it better!

## CHOCOLATE CINNAMON CAKE

Gather Up: Butter, Water, Cocoa Powder, Sugar, Flour, 2 Eggs, Ground Cinnamon, Buttermilk, Baking Soda, Milk, Powdered Sugar and Vanilla

In a Medium Sauce Pan Melt on Low heat on top of stove:

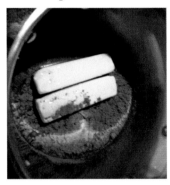 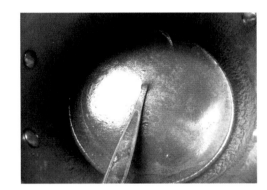

    2 Sticks of Butter (1 Cup)

    1 Cup of water

    4 tablespoons of Cocoa

In a Large Bowl Mix:

    2 Cups of Sugar

    2 Cups of Flour (all purpose or Ultragrain)

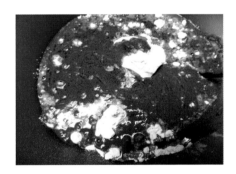

Add Sauce Pan mixture to Sugar-Flour Bowl and Mix

Add:

    2 Eggs

    ½ teaspoon of Ground Cinnamon

In a measuring Cup mix:

    ½ Cup of Buttermilk

    1 teaspoon of Baking Soda

Pour into Large Sugar-Flour- Cocoa- Butter mixture bowl and beat for 2 minutes with a handheld electric mixer.

Pour into a Steamer Pan sprayed with Pam. Bake at 350 degrees for 40 minutes.

Poke Holes in the top of the cake with a wooden toothpick or shish kabob skewer when cake is done.

Cool for 10 minutes.

Pour Chocolate Fudge Frosting on top of cake.

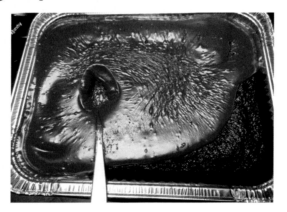

Chocolate Fudge Frosting:

In the same Medium Saucepan you used to make the cake melt:

> 1 Stick of Butter (1/2 Cup)
>
> 4 Tablespoons of Cocoa
>
> 6 Tablespoons of Milk

Mix in:

> 4 Cups of Powdered Sugar (1 Box)
>
> 1 teaspoon of Vanilla

Beat with a metal Spoon until it is Shiny and thick.

Pour on cooled cake.

Chocolate Sin Cake is the Ultimate Year Round Shipper. It is rich and decadent but not too sweet. I have seen some form of this recipe in several different church cookbooks and the cooks name was always preceded by Granny. Chocolate Sin Cake stays moist for weeks in a Tupperware container. This Cake can also be topped with Cool Whip or, better yet, real whipped cream! Topping with Vanilla Ice Cream, Hot Fudge and Real Whipped Cream is the BOMB!

# CHOCOLATE SIN CAKE

Gather Up: Butter, Sugar, 6 Eggs, Vanilla, Milk, Chocolate Graham Crackers, Shredded Coconut, Semi-Sweet Chocolate Chips, Heath Bar "Bits of Brickle" Chips

In a Large Bowl Mix:

   1 Cup of Butter Softened (2 Sticks)

   2 Cups of Sugar

   6 Large Eggs (Beat in one at a time)

   1 Teaspoon of Vanilla

   ½ Cup of Milk

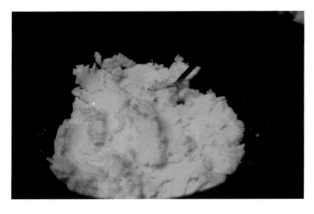 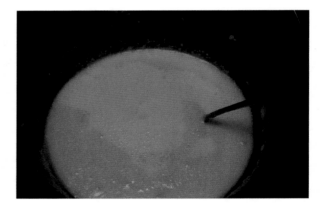

Fold in:

   4 Cups of Crushed, Chocolate Graham Crackers (2 sleeves and 4 additional crackers)

1 Cup of Finely Shredded Sweetened Coconut

½ Cup of Semi- Sweet Chocolate Chips

½ Cup of Heath Bar (Bits of Brickle)

1/4 Cup of Bourbon (optional)

Pour into a Steamer Pan which has been sprayed with Pam.

Bake at 350 degrees for 1 Hour.

Cool.

Dust with Powdered Sugar.

Overnight Monkey Bread is not a cake and more of a breakfast item, but all of my kids and their friends love this one. And it is sooo easy to make. Every school cookbook has several versions of Monkey Bread using canned biscuits. Those recipes are ok but not Delicious. This is a recipe using frozen bread balls and is from a mom of one of my younger son's friends, who put it in the school/church cookbook. It is Incredible! It involves putting frozen bread balls in a bundt pan and pouring a mixture of cinnamon, sugar, caramel pudding mix (dry) and a stick of melted butter. You then leave it overnight to raise and bake in the morning to serve it warm and gooie. One important point is to use regular Butterscotch or Caramel pudding mix NOT INSTANT. If you make it with instant pudding mix it's terrible! (I wanted this on my Birthday for Breakfast and only had only instant pudding mix. That's why I know it is TERRIBLE!) Another important point is to mix everything together and then pour it over the bread balls. Last but not least is leave it overnight in the microwave that way it won't dry out as it raises. Just remember you have it in the microwave so Don't Turn the Microwave On! I flip it over in a Steamer Pan and ship it to my kids.

# OVERNIGHT MONKEY BREAD

Gather Up: Chopped Pecans, frozen dinner rolls (balls), sugar, butterscotch pudding mix, ground cinnamon and butter

Spray A Bundt Pan with Pam.

Sprinkle ½ cup of Chopped or Whole Pecans in the bottom of the pan

Layer 1 (24 oz) package of Frozen(dinner rolls) Bread Balls in the bottom of the Pan

In a small bowl Mix:

    3/4 Cup of Sugar

    1 (3 ½ oz) package of Butterscotch/ Caramel Pudding mix (NOT INSTANT!)

    1 teaspoon of Ground Cinnamon

Sprinkle over the top of the Bread Balls.

Melt 1 Stick plus 2 Tablespoons of Butter and pour over Bread Balls.

Cover loosely and let sit out overnight (May leave in the Microwave to retain moisture but don't forget it's there!)

*In the Morning* Bake at 350 degrees for 25 minutes.

Let Cool for 10 minutes and then invert pan onto a serving plate. Or a Steamer Pan for Shipping!

 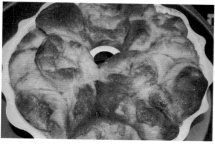 

Use a spoon to get out any remaining caramel stuck in the pan.

Serve with Cream Cheese frosting to dip pieces in!

I first tasted these peanut butter brownies when the mother of one of my patients gave me a Tupperware full of them after the successful birth of her grandson. It was late at night and I don't know if I was so tired and hungry that anything would have tasted incredible, but these did! She knew I would ask for the recipe because she had it taped to the box. These are very moist and easy to make.

## PEANUT BUTTER BROWNIES with CHOCOLATE PEANUT BUTTER FROSTING

Gather Up: Peanut Butter, Softened Butter, Brown Sugar, Vanilla, 4 Eggs, and Flour, peanut butter Chips

In a Large Bowl Mix:

    1 Cup of Peanut Butter (Creamy or Chunky)

    ½ Cup of softened Butter (1 Stick)

    2 Cup of packed Brown Sugar

    2 teaspoon of Vanilla

    4 Eggs

Add:

    1 1/3 Cup of Flour (All Purpose or Ultragrain)

Stir In:

1 Cup of Peanut Butter Chips

Pour into a Steamer Pan sprayed with Pam and Bake at 350 degrees for 40 minutes.

PEANUT BUTTER LOVERS FROSTING option 1 For People who LOVE Peanut Butter, but dislike Chocolate or any mixture of the 2! This is VERY PEAUNUT BUTTERY FROSTING! Year Round Shipper

Gather Up: Peanut Butter and Powdered Sugar

In a Medium Bowl Mix:

　　1 Cup of Peanut Butter (Creamy or Chunky) (If you use creamy in brownies then use chunky in frosting or vice versa.

　　½ Cup of Powdered Sugar

PEANUT BUTTER FROSTING option 2 This is for people who LOVE Peanut Butter, but dislike Chocolate or any mixture of the 2! And like a Lighter Peanut Butter Frosting.

Gather Up: 1 Can White Frosting and Peanut Butter. Year Round Shipper

In a Medium Bowl Heat in the Microwave for 1 minute on High:

　　1 Can of White Frosting

Add:

　　1 Cup of Peanut Butter (Creamy or Chunky)

Spread warm onto warm Peanut Butter Bars

CHOCOLATE PEANUT BUTTER FROSTING option 3 This is a wonderful Chocolate Peanut Butter taste!

And Also a Great Chocolate Peanut Butter Fudge by itself! Year Round Shipper.

Gather Up: 1 can Chocolate Frosting and Peanut Butter

In a Medium Bowl Heat in the Microwave for 1 minute on High:

　　1 Can of Chocolate Frosting

Add:

　　1 Cup of Peanut Butter (Creamy or Chunky - I like chunky the best!)

Pour on cooled brownies.

I love to ship Bars and most of my cookie recipes I make as Bars for this very reason. The Rolo Bars are my favorites. They are easy to make and Awesome. I just make my chocolate chip cookie recipe and spread them in a Steamer Pan. Then 10 minutes into the baking I pull the pan out and push into the cookie bars a whole package of unwrapped Rolo Bars so just the tops are visible. I then bake them for 30 more minutes. I just love biting into them and getting a mouthful of chocolate and gooie caramel! My son Carter loves these made with Reese peanut butter cups. Both are Year Round Shippers.

## ROLO BARS

Gather Up: Butter, light brown Sugar, Flour, 4 Eggs, Vanilla, Baking Powder, Semi-Sweet Chocolate Chips and 1 package of Mini, Unwrapped Rolo Candy

In a Large Mixing Bowl Mix:

> 1/2Cup of Softened Butter (1 Stick)
>
> 2 Cups of Packed light Brown Sugar
>
> 4 Large Eggs

Add:

> 2 1/2 Cups of Flour (All Purpose)
>
> 2 teaspoons of Baking Powder
>
> 1 Cup of Chocolate Chips Semi-Sweet
>
> 2 teaspoons of Vanilla

Press Batter with your fingers into a Steam Pan sprayed with Pam.

Bake at 350 degrees for 10 minutes.

  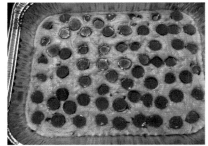

Remove from Oven and Press one bag of Mini Unwrapped Rolo Candy into the tops of cookie bars evenly spacing Rolo Candy.

Return to Oven for 30 minutes.

Cool 30 minutes and cut into bars.

Rolo Candy can be replaced with a bag of Mini Unwrapped Reese Peanut Butter Cups or Hershey Kisses with Caramel also. I recently used my kids uneaten Christmas Candy in March! I had put Hershey Kisses with Caramel centers and Reese Peanut Butter Cup bells in their Christmas Stockings. They had poured them into a bowl in the living room and forgot about them. In March I saw all these Green, Red and Gold wrapped candy and thought "What Should I Do"? They were still good but no one would eat them close to Easter! So I made the Rolo Cookie Bars and instead unwrapped all the Christmas Candy and pushed them in! My Staff devoured these! Now I know what candy to put in their Easter Baskets! I do not recommend Snickers. The Snickers do not keep their taste and harden very quickly in the bars. I also ship Easter Baskets to my kids in college. Another Book option?

Another favorite shipper is Brownies. This recipe is very RICH just looking at the ingredients. This is a GREAT Brownie Recipe but I absolutely love the Hershey's and Giaradelli's Brownie mixes too. Using these you can be so creative! My favorite is the Rocky Road Brownies. With these, you bake the brownies as directed. When they are done, pull them out and put a 7 oz package of mini marshmallows covering the top. Bake the brownies for 10 more minutes. Then I let them cool down and pour Chocolate Fudge Frosting over the marshmallows. These are a hit anyplace I take them and ship well! For people who like Mint, taking them out of the oven and placing a box of York Peppermint Patties on top and swirling them after they melt is an excellent option. I also like frosting them with different frostings like Coconut Pecan, Cream Cheese or Chocolate and then topping the frosting with mini chocolate chips, nuts, Heath Bar chips, chopped Reeses's or Snicker's. A Brownie Sundae without the Icecream!

# HEAVENLY RICH CHOCOLATE BROWNIES

Gather Up: Butter, Unsweetened Chocolate Bars, Sugar, Flour, 6 Eggs, semi-sweet Chocolate Chips and Vanilla

In a Medium Saucepan Melt on the Stovetop:

    1 1/2 Cups of Butter

    6 oz of Unsweetened Chocolate

In a Large Mixing Bowl Mix:

    3 Cups of Sugar

    1 ½ Cup of Flour

Add Chocolate mixture to Sugar-Flour Mixture

Add:

  6 Large Eggs

  2 teaspoons of Vanilla

Fold in 2 Cups of Chocolate Chips (semi-sweet)

Spread in a Steamer Pan sprayed with Pam and Bake at 325 degrees for 50 minutes.

Cool at least 30 minutes before cutting.


ROCKY ROAD BROWNIES

Gather Up: 1 pan of Baked Brownies (just out of the oven), 1 small package of Mini Marshmallows, Butter, Cocoa, Milk, Powdered Sugar and Vanilla

Spread marshmallows on top of hot brownies.

Put them back in the oven at 350 degrees for 10 minutes.

Cool 10 minutes and pour chocolate fudge frosting evenly over the marshmallows.

Cool before Cutting.

# CHOCOLATE FUDGE FROSTING

In a Medium Sauce pan Melt:

>    1 Stick of Butter (1/2 Cup)

>    4 Tablespoons of Cocoa

>    6 Tablespoons of Milk

Mix In:

>    4 Cups of Powdered Sugar (1 Box)

>    1 teaspoon of Vanilla

Beat with a metal spoon until it is shiny and thick.

Pour over marshmallows on top of brownies

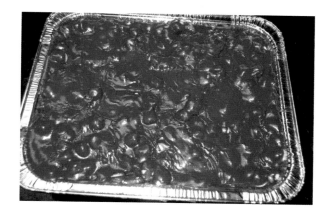

Granny D's Turtle Bars are another favorite of mine and my older sister, Christine. Granny D always made these at Christmas Time but I think they are GREAT anytime. They are very sweet and difficult to make because the caramel has to come out perfect or they are too hard. My Sister makes these every Christmas and gives them away as presents in very ornate Christmas tins.

# GRANNY D'S TURTLE BARS

Gather Up: Flour, Light Brown Sugar, Butter, Pecan Halves, finely chopped Pecans, and Milk Chocolate Chips

In a Medium Mixing Bowl Mix with Forks or a Pastry Blender:

    2 Cups of Flour

    1 Cup of Light Brown Sugar packed

    1 Stick of Butter (1/2 Cup) Hard

    ½ Cup finely chopped Pecans

Press in a Steamer Pan Sprayed with Pam.

Pour over Crust:

    1 Cup of Pecan Halves

In a Medium Saucepan Mix:

    1 1/3 Cup of Butter

    1 Cup of Brown Sugar

Bring to a Boil and Stir constantly with a metal or wood spoon for 2 minutes. It should be creamy. Do Not Use a Whisk!!!!

Pour over Pecans.

Bake in a 350 degree oven for 20 minutes. Do Not Overbake!

Remove from oven and:

Pour 2 Cups of Milk Chocolate Chips over the Hot Baked Crust. When Chips are melted spread with a knife.

Cool at least 1 hour before cutting.

 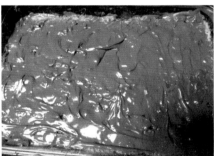 

Another year round shipping bar cookie are the White Chocolate and Craisin Oatmeal Bars. These are delicious and keep for weeks.

# WHITE CHOCOLATE AND CRAISIN OATMEAL BARS

Gather Up: White chocolate Chips, Craisins, Butter, Light Brown Sugar, Sugar, Eggs, Vanilla, Flour, Baking Soda, Ground Cinnamon, Salt, Quaker Old Fashioned uncooked Oats

In a Large Mixing Bowl Cream:

> ¾ Cup of Soft Butter
>
> ¾ Cup of Sugar
>
> ¾ Cup of packed Light Brown Sugar

Mix In:

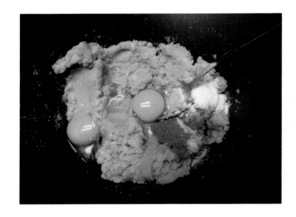

> 2 Eggs
>
> ½ teaspoon of Salt
>
> 1 ½ Cups of All –Purpose Flour (or Ultragrain)
>
> 1 teaspoon of Baking Soda
>
> 1 teaspoon of Vanilla

Add:

> 3 Cups of Old Fashioned uncooked Oats
>
> 1 Cup of White Chocolate Chips
>
> 1 Cup of Craisins

Pour Batter into a Steamer Pan Sprayed with Pam. Push dough down with your fingers.

Bake at 350 degrees for 45 Minutes

These Dumplings are in hundreds of cookbooks but I tweak them a little to make them even better than Incredible and faster to make. I use Fresh Peaches and leave the skin on. Peeling a peach is hard to do and very unnecessary! The important points are to use real Mountain Dew and NOT DIET. I use a whole quarter of a Peach for each dumpling and Grand Crescent Rolls (the BIG ones!). The sauce the Mountain Dew makes is another one of those eat –with- a- spoon glazes! Of course these can also be made the traditional way using 2 large Granny Smith Apples. Year Round Shipper.

# MOUNTAIN DEW PEACH DUMPLINGS

Gather Up: 2 Large Fresh Peaches, 1 Can of Grand Crescent Rolls, Sugar, Ground Cinnamon, Butter and (1) 12 oz can of Mountain Dew

Peel, Cut, take out Pit and Cut into Quarters 2 Large Fresh Peaches

Roll out 1 Can of Grand, Crescent Rolls

Wrap each Peach Quarter in a Triangle of Crescent Roll.

Lay 8 sections evenly spaced in a Steamer Pan.

In a Small Bowl Melt in the Microwave:

   ¾ Cup of Butter (1 ½ Sticks)

Add:

   1 Cup of Sugar

   1 teaspoon of Ground Cinnamon

Pour Mixture Evenly over Peach Quarters

Pour 1 12oz can of Mountain Dew over Peach Quarters

Bake at 350 degrees for 45 minutes

Enjoy warm with Cinnamon Ice Cream or Vanilla Ice Cream spooning the Dumpling Syrup over Ice Cream

This is a year round shipper

Caramel Apple Pie is one of those desserts I can take anywhere and it will be gone in minutes! They are eaten so fast that I usually make 2 or 3 at a time. My younger son, Carter, has several friends that love this pie so I can make 3 and an hour later come downstairs to find all three missing! Carter likes to hand out my Caramel Apple Pies! I have started making these in Steamer Pans and shipping them. All caramel is not made equally. I favor Smuckers, Berrymans or Marzetti's Caramel Dip. Cheap Caramel is too runny! When you have to peel, Core and Chop 10 apples at a time I get the Hand Crank Apple Peeler, Corer and Slicer machine out! I have made a whole recipe of my Buttermilk Pie Crust and laid it in a Steamer Pan, poured the apple mixture in the crust and topped with crumb topping. Caramel is drizzled on when the "Pie" is cooled. This can feed a large party! Year Round Shipper

# CARAMEL APPLE PIE

Gather Up: 1 buttermilk pie crust recipe, 10 Large Granny Smith Apples, Flour, Ground Cinnamon, Sugar, Whipping Cream, Vanilla, Butter, Salt, Chopped Pecans and Caramel Ice Cream Topping or Apple Dip

Peel, Core and Slice 10 large Granny Smith Apples

 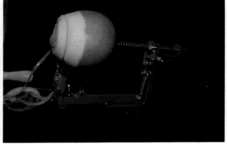 

In a Large Bowl Add to Apples:

    6 Tablespoons of Flour

    2 teaspoon of Ground Cinnamon

    2 Cup of Sugar

    2 Tablespoon of Cream

    2 teaspoon of Vanilla

    2 Tablespoons of melted Butter

Pour into a Buttermilk Pie Crust unbaked in a Steamer Pan

In a Small Bowl Mix:

    3 Cups of Flour

    20 Tablespoons of Melted Butter

    ½ Cup of Sugar

    ½ Cup of Light Brown Sugar

    ½ teaspoon of Salt

    1 Cup of Chopped Fine Pecans

Sprinkle over Apple Mixture and bake pie at 350 degrees for 1 hour and 20 minutes.

When Pie is Cool Drizzle with Caramel.

You can ship this Year Round.

At this point I have to get serious about pie crust. For years my Grandma O'Connor baked and baked. She was a cook at the local hospital in Dansville, NY where she lived. She baked for all the hospital special events and probably made over a million Petit Fours in her 83 years. Petit Fours are a lost art and have probably been replaced with cake pops. When I was young, I remember traveling in a Station Wagon car with my parents and 3 siblings for hours arriving in Dansville at two in the morning. We were greeted by Grandma O'Connor and a huge spread of food including roast beef, ham, turkey, mashed potatoes, hot rolls and usually five or six pies. Her pie crust was always so flaky! When I was 16, I drove my little sister Cindy 8 ½ hours in my Triumph Spitfire deathtrap to Grandma O'Connor's. There we spent a week baking with her. She would bake in her kitchen and send me upstairs to her second kitchen to whip up cookies. We then traveled around town dropping gifts to all her friends. She used to make these delicious Caramel Pecan yeast rolls that were incredible. The aroma would make your stomach gurgle. She always had dough in the refrigerator so she could whip up a batch with 20 minutes notice! She also did this with her pancake dough which made the fluffiest pancakes you could ever eat. I don't have these recipes or her pie crust recipe although I'm sure it would have consisted of 4 handfuls of this and a splash of that! I do remember she always added buttermilk to her flour mixture for pie crust. This is the closest recipe I have found. When I am crunched for time I do use the store-bought variety which will suffice especially if it's only the bottom crust. I really like Aldi's brand Bakehouse Creations. It is flaky and doesn't get tough and shiny if you use it for a top crust the way some other brands do.

## BUTTERMILK PIE CRUST

Gather Up: All Purpose Flour, Vegetable Shortening, Butter and Buttermilk

Mix with Pastry Blender or Fork:

> 3 Cups of (Sifted) All Purpose Flour

> 1 Cup of Shortening

> 4 Tablespoons of Butter (hard)

When crumbly the size of peas then mix in 1/2 Cup of cold Buttermilk (not low fat)

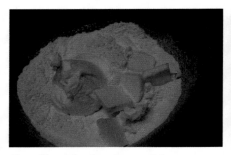

Handle as little as possible.

Scoop dough into a Ball with floured hands and cut ball in half.

Roll out each half on a floured board for one crust.

This recipe is very ample for a two crust pie but I always like to have too much rather than too little!

A Steamer Pan takes a whole recipe for one layer!

You cannot be from Tennessee without making a Bourbon Chocolate Pecan Pie. The hardest decision to make is what brand of Bourbon Whiskey to use. I tend not to cook with the Tennessee Moonshine Whiskey variety or Scotch. I favor more the likes of Jack Daniels of Lynchburg, Tennessee. The Whiskey Trail is in neighboring Kentucky and includes 5 of the nation's most famous brands. The Kentucky Whiskey Trail was created in 1999 and includes Four Roses and Wild Turkey near Lawrenceburg, Heaven Hill at Bardstown, Jim Beam at Clermont, Markers Mark at Loretto and Woodford Reserve near Versailles. I like to use Wild Turkey in my cooking creations but my husband favors Makers Mark 46 and my son Meade loves Woodford Reserve. My probable future Son-In-Law, and first Editor, Luke, drinks Buffalo Trace on the rocks! My brother in law John made the Bourbon Chocolate Pecan Pie last Thanksgiving for the first time and my brother John (I have 2 brother in laws and 1 brother named John! A little confusing?) texted me that it was "Bourbon Chocolate Ecstasy!" I suspect my brother-in- law increased the normal amount of Bourbon, and they are the Wild Turkey lovers of the family. My Dad likes Wild Turkey or John Jameson (Irish whiskey) in his Whiskey Cakes I ship to him. He likes to remind me that Whisky is from the Gaelic, "water of life". I have one brother-in- law, Alec, who would probably have me use Eagles Rare 17 or Pappys! (If you know anything about Bourbon then you know that these two run about 500.00 a bottle which makes for a very pricey pie which uses almost a cup of liquor!) If you don't like Chocolate then leave the Chocolate chips out of the following recipe and this leaves a Bourbon Pecan Pie. You can also leave just leave the Bourbon out and you will have a Chocolate Pecan Pie. I know you are thinking "she is shipping alcohol to minors??? No, the alcohol burns off during cooking leaving the flavor.

## BOURBON CHOCOLATE PECAN PIE

Gather Up: 1 Buttermilk Pie Crust unbaked, Sugar, Light Corn Syrup, Butter, Semi-Sweet Chocolate Chips, 8 Eggs, Salt, Pecan Halves and last but not least Bourbon

In a Medium Saucepan Melt:

> 2 Cup Sugar

> 2 Cup of Light Corn Syrup

> 2/3 Cup of Butter

> 2/3 Cup of Chocolate Chips (Semi-Sweet)

Mix with a whisk. This should be creamy.

Add to Chocolate Mixture mixing with Whisk: 8 Large Eggs Beaten, 1/2 teaspoon Salt, 1/2 Cup of Bourbon Pour into 1 unbaked Buttermilk Pie Crust pressed in a Steamer Pan. Cover Top of Filling with 2 1/2 Cups of Pecan Halves.

Bake at 325 degrees for 1 hour and 20 minutes. Cool and Serve warm with Whipped Cream. Wrap tightly with Plastic Wrap and then top with a metal top for Shipping. Year Round Shipper

Cowboy cookies have almost anything you can think of thrown in a cookie. One of my patients brought them in to my office when she came in for her post partum exam. My girls loved them so I got the recipe. Almost any school, church or work cookbook you buy will have some form of these cookies. I have seen them called Cowboy Cookies, Monster Cookies, Trash Cookies, Garbage Cookies and so on. They have something in them for everyone, are great and ship well. I have made these as Bars, but I think they taste better as Cookies. Beware anyone with food allergies! These are Year Round Shippers.

# COWBOY COOKIES

Gather Up: Butter, Sugar, Dark Brown Sugar, 3 Eggs, Peanut Butter, Vanilla, Old Fashioned Oats, Semi-Sweet Chocolate Chips, Baking Soda, White Chocolate Chips, Raisins and Chopped Walnuts

In a Large Mixing Bowl Mix:

> ½ Cup of Softened Butter (1 Stick)

> 1 Cup of Sugar

> 1 Cup and 2 Tablespoons of Dark Brown Sugar Packed

Mix in:

> 3 Large Eggs

> 2 Cups of Peanut Butter (Creamy or Chunky) I like Creamy in these cookies!

> 1 teaspoon of Vanilla

Add:

> 4 ½ Cups of Regular Old Fashioned Oats

> 2 teaspoons of Baking Soda

 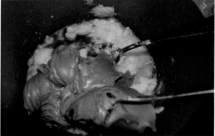 

Stir in:

> 1 ½ Cups of Chocolate Chips (Semi-Sweet)

> ½ Cup of White Chocolate Chips

> ½ Cup of Raisins

> ½ Cup of Chopped walnuts

Spray Cookie Sheet with Pam and drop Cookie Dough onto Sheet with a sprayed ¼ Cup measuring cup.

Bake at 350 degrees for 15 minutes.

Cool first on the cookie sheet before removing. If they are too hot they will fall apart!

I have also made these as Bars. Spread batter with your fingers in a Pam Sprayed Steamer Pan and bake at 325 degrees for 1 hour. These are very thick Bars.

For 13 years my 3 children attended a small private school in Knoxville called Tate's School of Discovery. This school goes from the 3 year olds to fifth grade and is situated on a Christmas Tree Farm. Every year they have a Halloween Carnival which my good friend Rhonda chaired for at least 10 years. The Jack o lantern Trail through the woods is worth going back each year to see even though my last child graduated 7 years ago. I used to just help out wherever I was needed for the Carnival. The Bake Sale attracted hundreds of donations some of which were Awesome. Fran's Fruit Bars were one of those items. The grandmother of one of the students made these every year. When that student graduated everyone asked where the Fruit Bars were! When the school decided to put together a cookbook I tracked down Fran and got the recipe. When I recently baked these my 21 year old daughter took one bite and exclaimed "Tate's Carnival!" These Ship well and even if they end up in pieces every piece is eaten according to my children! Year Round Shipper.

# FRANS FRUIT BARS

Gather Up: Butter, Sugar, 3 Eggs, Baking Powder, Water, (1) 8 oz package of Chopped Dates, Flour, Ground Cinnamon, Nutmeg, Ground Cloves, Salt and Chopped Pecans

In a Large Mixing Bowl Cream:

> 1 Cup of Softened Butter (2 Sticks)

> 2 Cups of Sugar

Add :

> 3 Large Eggs one at a time and mix.

Add :

> 1 teaspoon of Baking Powder

> 1 teaspoon of Water

Add:

> 1 Package of Chopped Dates (8oz)

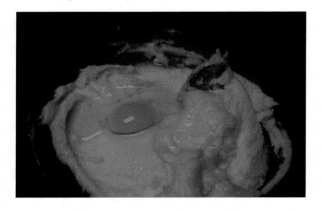
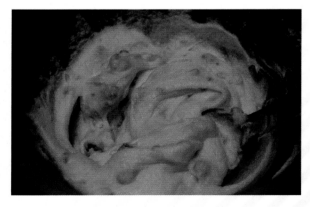

Mix In:

3 Cups of Flour (Sifted All Purpose)

1 Teaspoon of Ground Cinnamon

1 Teaspoon of Nutmeg

½ Teaspoon of ground Cloves

1/8 Teaspoon of Salt

1 Cup of Chopped Pecans

Chill Dough for 2 Hours.

On Floured Board Shape Dough into (3) 10 inch long Rolls that are 2 Inches in Diameter.

Place Rolls on a Baking Sheet sprayed with Pam. No more than 2 rolls per baking sheet

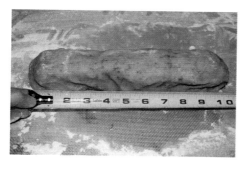 

Press down on the Rolls with your fingers to flatten the dough a little.

Sprinkle Rolls with 3 teaspoons of Sugar. 1 teaspoon per roll.

Bake at 325 degrees for 25 minutes.

While still hot, cut Rolls into Diagonal Strips 1 ½ inches apart.

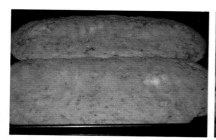  

# INSPIRATION

## PEOPLE

Mom (Constance Grace Wood O'Connor 1935-2008)

Grandma O'Connor (Evelyn Augusta Gousha 1903-1987)

Granny D (Clara Bohan Wood Devlin 1915-1996)

Christine Coughlin (my big sister)

Rhonda Wilson

Melinda Kennard RN

Mary Constantine Knoxville News Sentinel

## COOK BOOKS

Betty Crocker's Cookbook 2000

Faith, Family and Food Sacred Heart Cathedral Cookbook

Nestle Classic Recipes 2003

Our Best Recipes from Tate's School of Discovery 2003

The Redbook Cookbook 1971

Printed in the United States
By Bookmasters